THE STORY OF
GHOST TOWN
CARIBOU

At its peak, Caribou boasted of a bustling business community that included saloons, churches, mercantiles, a telegraph office, and a school. The photographer who created this stereograph was standing on Goat Hill.

Nederland Area Historical Society, Buchanan Collection

THE STORY OF
GHOST TOWN
—⚡—
CARIBOU

JOHN W. BUCHANAN
and
DORIS G. BUCHANAN

© 2024 Nederland Area Historical Society

ALL RIGHTS RESERVED. No part of this book may be reproduced without written permission from the publisher, except in the case of brief excerpts in critical reviews and articles. Address all inquiries to: Nederland Area Historical Society, PO Box 1252, Nederland, Colorado 80466.

ISBN 978-0-9753711-1-4

First Edition 1957
Second Edition 2024

Cover photo: Nederland Area Historical Society, Buchanan Collection

The wind swept down on her from the Roof of the World. The snow drifted higher than houses. The mines on the hills hoisted millions of dollars in silver ore.

To her came the restless ones from the deep tin mines of Cornwall, from the fair green hills of Ireland, from the gale-swept coast of Nova Scotia, from the far-flung frontier of America. Named for an Arctic animal that pawed its food from beneath the frozen snow, she was a mining camp at once strange and wondrous.

In short, she was Caribou.

—Forest Crossen, author of *Western Yesterdays*

CONTENTS

Foreword.....1

Preface.....5

Introduction.....9

CHAPTER ONE.....15
The Legend of Treasure Mountain

CHAPTER TWO.....21
Scratch of the Pick

CHAPTER THREE.....39
Where the Winds Were Born

CHAPTER FOUR.....55
The Boom and The Bust

EPILOGUE.....77

BIBLIOGRAPHY.....83

FOREWORD

This book had its start as a thirty-six-page booklet published in 1957 by John and Doris Buchanan.

The booklet incorporated a series of articles about Caribou that had been published in the Boulder Daily Camera in 1944, when they were both working at the newspaper. Many of the mining camp's former residents and business owners who were still living responded to the series, and the Camera was flooded with letters and interviews, all of which were published. John did some of the interviews and helped edit the letters and reminiscences the Camera received. He even ghostwrote some of them. That flood of responses proved so popular that John and Doris decided to collect the articles into a booklet.

Both John and Doris had life-long connections to Boulder, Nederland, and Caribou. Doris's mother was born near Fort Collins, and as a teenager her mother worked in a boardinghouse in Lakewood, the tungsten camp just north of Nederland. She met Doris's father while working at another

Doris Buchanan and Benjie visited Caribou in the summer of 1968, and their photo appeared in a story John wrote about Caribou for the Denver Post's Empire magazine in December of that year. While he worked at the Post, John both wrote and broadcast stories. Here, Ed Lehman holds a broadcast script for him on Nov. 5, 1949, in Denver.

Denver Public Library Special Collections, X-28836

boardinghouse on Sugarloaf. Walter Frank Gardner was a miner, a hoist man who worked at several of the area's tungsten mines, including the Friday mine on Sugarloaf. Doris's parents were married in 1914, and they lived for a while in a tent on Sugarloaf near the mines. Doris was conceived in that tent, and her mother recalled taking the narrow gauge train to Boulder to give birth.

Doris was born in Boulder in 1917. In yet another connection to the history of Caribou, Dr. Carbon Gillaspie, who had previously served as Nederland's and Caribou's doctor, was her mother's doctor and delivered Doris.

Doris married the year before she got out of high school, and as soon as she graduated she and her husband moved to Vermont, but they didn't like it and soon came back to Colorado. They divorced soon after that, and she moved in with her mother.

Doris learned midwifery from her mother, and the two of them ran a convalescent home in Boulder where pregnant women and old-timers from the Boulder area, including Caribou, often stayed. They closed the home in 1939, and Doris started work at the Boulder Daily Camera, where she met John Buchanan.

John had graduated from the University of Colorado School of Journalism in 1940, and his first job was with the Boulder Daily Camera where he met Doris. They were married in 1942. John was exempted from service in the military during World War II and stayed in Boulder. He worked lots of extra hours because so many of the men at the newspaper were fighting the war. In addition to his other duties at the Camera, he wrote editorials, and many of them were award-winning. In 1945, his editorials captured the attention of Palmer Hoyt, the new publisher of The Denver Post, who offered John a job.

John spent fifteen years at the Post as city hall reporter and writing a weekly city hall column. In 1965 he joined the staff of Empire, the paper's Sunday magazine, where he wrote a weekly column full of folksy recollections and humor, with an occasional foray into politics. He was known for his meticulous work and as a practical joker. He became the assistant editor for Empire and retired in 1985.

Early in their marriage, Doris, a child of the Depression, as John put it, insisted that they must have a house of their own. They bought a miner's cabin on Big Springs Drive in Nederland for which they put $10 down and paid $10 a month. Eventually they replaced the cabin with a new structure and spent many happy hours exploring the history of the Nederland area.

John and Doris were Western history buffs, and they published booklets on the old Windsor Hotel and the ghost town of Caribou. The Caribou booklet was published in 1957.

John died at the age of 84 in 2003, and Doris died in 2005 at the age of 87. They bequeathed the rights to *The Story of Ghost Town Caribou* to the Nederland Area Historical Society.

That's how this book was born—it started with their original manuscript and photographs, most of which were taken by John. We added some vignettes from the stories that were originally published in the Boulder Daily Camera in 1944 and brought the mining camp's history up to date.

We will be forever grateful to Doris and John, those fervent guardians of our area's history, who originally brought this story of ghost town Caribou to life.

—Kay Turnbaugh
for the Nederland Area Historical Society

PREFACE

Some states can tell their history in monuments. Others write their story in battlefields. And some pen their past in cities and in buildings.

Colorado's early history is written in part by its ghost towns. A bleak and windswept mountain ridge or valley has often been the burial ground for an early-day mining camp.

These ghost towns, now so dead, witnessed a lust for life rarely equaled in the annals of the history of our country. They were home to the fur trapper, the miner, and the scout—a breed who came and went. These were the people who founded the state of Colorado and who lingered within its territorial borders only so long as it offered them the best possible place in the world to play their particular game of cards.

They were a courageous, swashbuckling, hard-working, hard-playing, restless assemblage. They headed confidently for the next bend in the stream, around which surely outcropped the mother lode.

Towns materialized instantly, going through a rapid progress from campfire to tent, from tent to log cabin, from cabin to frame structure, and then to brick or stone. These early mining towns were connected to civilization by a thin and tenuous cord that somehow carried lurching wagon trains into the granite heart of the Rocky Mountains.

Colorado's early mining towns materialized under a wand of gold.

They grew rapidly. Some became firmly established, sending roots deep into the mountains that spawned them. Many died fast, sparkling into a brief flame of life, then flickering into the dust of centuries.

The true Colorado ghost town burned briefly. Like the miner and the trapper it moved flamboyantly and quickly onto center stage, and then drifted into off-stage oblivion.

This is the story of one of these ghost towns, Caribou.

—John W. and Doris G. Buchanan

These women donned their best dresses and posed for a photographer who visited Caribou on a sunny summer day, probably in the 1870s.

Nederland Area Historical Society

One of the few remaining structures in Caribou in the 1940s was the Post Office.
Nederland Area Historical Society, Buchanan Collection

INTRODUCTION

Town of Ghosts
1957

No one lives there now.

Scattered on top of the hill are bones of what was once a shaft house. They are whitened by the sun and picked clean by a hungry and howling wind which scours the mountainside perpetually.

The bones of the town of Caribou slowly mingle with the dust of eternity.

A dozen warped and decaying houses stand askew in the lap of the hill and furnish residence only for families of pack rats that scurry into twisted rafters on hearing the intruder's step.

Gallows frames, creaking in the wind, straddle crumbling mine shafts.

The bleak, wild and windswept ridge is pocked with mine dumps scattered across its slopes like colossal graves.

Nearby, in a pine-forested swale rimmed on the west by Old Baldy peak and the Continental Divide, is the burial ground of the people.

The people are gone. The homes, the stores, the boardwalks, and the mine buildings they once fashioned have crumbled. Only a gaunt and twisted handful of these timbered structures hang to the mountainside like wrinkled October apples from the tree. Each year one more, after battling the whip-saw of winter winds and the crushing weight of snow, surrenders with a wrenching groan to the relentless conquerors.

The mines are but scars now. Crumbling rock fills the deeper wounds of the hillside.

Listen and you can hear the sounds of eternity—a rumble of distant thunder tumbles off the burly shoulders of a far-away mountain peak; wind whispers through gnarled timberline trees; a pebble rustles, dislodged from a mine dump by the infinite patience of gravity.

These are the sounds of Caribou—of the storms that lash mountain ranges into flat prairies; of the winds that slowly lick away the granite walls.

Only these elemental things are there—and the ghosts of yesteryear, the ghosts of a brawling crowd of adventure-seekers whose Pied Piper was the show of color in rustling gold pans.

They alone are inhabitants of this town—ghosts of the Shoo-Fly dance hall; of Cousin Jack pasties; of the drifting odor of fried potatoes and onions greeting a miner at

An abandoned hoist engine at Caribou.

Nederland Area Historical Society, Edgeley W. Todd Collection

A few buildings in Caribou had managed to survive when authors John and Doris Buchanan wrote their book about the town. Even these gradually succumbed to time and the harsh elements.

Nederland Area Historical Society, Buchanan Collection

his home; ghosts of blue pine smoke fingering the winter sky from a red brick chimney; ghosts of gumboots thumping along a boardwalk.

Occasionally an automobile whines up the Coon Trail. Strangers step out and guess that this must be the site of the town—strangers drawn to the spot that once seethed in the electric adventure of their forebears.

This, like a photograph stained and faded into grey nothingness, is Caribou today.

As you read this book, keep in mind that it was published in 1957, and most of it was written in the 1940s. White Americans' view of Native Americans was not the same as it is now, and the fanciful depiction of the Native Americans who were living in the Nederland-Caribou area and their relationship with the early explorers and miners in Chapter 1 is an example of that difference.

Chapter One

The Legend of Treasure Mountain

The year was 1860.

Big tasks were ahead—a war to fight, a frontier to harness.

The young men who were to do this were working in factories and on farms east of the Mississippi River.

They were helping their fathers to put in crops, to clear the lower forty, to milk the cows. But many found time at night to turn up flickering lamps and read newspaper stories about a show of color on Cherry Creek in a territory called Kansas.

They read about the growth of a young frontier town called Denver City; of fabulous strikes in the Gregory Diggings west of Denver City.

This was happening in a territory where gold, game, Indians, and adventure jumped at you from every bend in the stream. This was the new American frontier. Here with a jar of sourdough, a flask of gunpowder, an axe, pick, and pan—and after a waterless, foodless trek across an expanse of prairie –you could carve yourself a fortune.

Wagon trains, "jumping off" from Missouri river towns, were carrying thousands of these adventure-seekers to the Pike's Peak gold regions.

One of these young men, Sam Conger, booked passage on such a prairie schooner armada.

Upon arriving in Denver, Conger listened awestruck to boasts of prospectors who picked into the hills a score of miles west of the confluence of Cherry Creek and the South Platte River.

He cocked his ear to the whispers of new finds, because whispers often write the pages of history where shouts fade out. He talked with army officers at the frontier city, and through them, so legend has it, met Bird Chief, war leader of the Arapahos.

Gold was the lure of Denver. Gold was the staff of this frontier life. Miners and prospectors had very few states' coins, and bargained with gold dust, so merchants had balance scales instead of money tills.

Most eyes looked for yellow dust. But young Sam Conger's gaze was drawn to the silver trinkets worn by the Arapahos, who were camped along the banks of Cherry Creek.

He questioned Bird Chief at length about the ornaments—so eagerly, so intently, and so frequently, in fact, that Bird Chief austerely shied away from the young man, suspecting him of plotting to make away with the tribe's silver wealth.

Conger theorized that the silver must be originating from somewhere near the Arapaho summer campground in a high mountain meadow along the banks of Middle Boulder Creek—a valley where the town of Nederland is now located.

Persistent conversation with the Arapahos elicited little information. But once or twice members of the tribe used the term "Treasure Mountain."

Conger became a hunter of wild game, rather than of yellow dust. He visited the Arapaho summer camp and talked about Treasure Mountain. During the summer he became closely associated with the Arapahos, and a warmer friendship grew between members of the tribe and this intruder. Even so, Conger was never able to get Bird Chief to talk about the silver ornaments.

There was a way.

Her name was Moaning Dove, daughter of Bird Chief and beautiful princess of the Arapahos. Moaning Dove listened when Conger, seated in her father's tepee, told stories of wonderful cities far across the plains to the east.

This friendship grew. There were exchanges of confidences, and one day Moaning Dove promised Conger she would show him Treasure Mountain. Surely the Arapahos had treasures to match the fabulous cities of the white man.

On the following night, Moaning Dove agreed, she would meet Conger at the western edge of the meadow on the trail to the high country. A two-hour stroll through the moonlight would show Conger the fabulous Treasure Mountain.

On that night Moaning Dove slipped from her tepee and quietly skimmed along the moonlit trail toward the edge of the meadow. A figure stepped out of the trees. It was not her white friend but her father, Bird Chief. There was no reprimand, no show of anger. Bird Chief stoically pointed back down the trail to the camp and Moaning Dove dutifully retraced her steps.

Conger paced back and forth in the moonlit meadow, and was so doing when Bird Chief arrived. The Indian chief still showed no anger. But he sternly reminded Conger that the young hunter was accepted in friendship by his people and must meet all of the obligations of that friendship.

As Conger sifted through the chief's allegorical enunciation, he concluded that were he to pursue the Treasure Mountain trail longer he would find death, rather than silver as his reward.

Conger pushed thoughts of Treasure Mountain from his mind for the time being.

One day the Arapahos trespassed into Ute hunting grounds, and the two tribes locked in battle. Both drew back bleeding, and the Arapahos moved on to other areas to find wild game.

Not until they left did Conger feel free to resume his search for Treasure Mountain. He was unskilled as a prospector, and he kept the secret mission to himself as he headed up the trails to the west. Weeks of scouring the hills for silver left him bone-weary. Through necessity he combined the job of hunting for silver with the task of hunting for game. It was exhausting work.

While he hunted one day he spotted an elk and began trailing it. The effort made his lungs pump hard, for he was

9,800 feet above sea level. The supply of oxygen in the air was lean.

He sat down on a rock to rest. As he wiped his brow and looked toward the east he saw what was later to be named Idaho Mountain. To the west was Caribou Hill. Ahead of him was Old Baldy, whose deeper clefts never shed all their snow even in the summertime.

Conger was about five miles west of what is now Nederland. He was sitting on the spot where the town of Caribou City would grow.

But Caribou Hill, exposing an abundant flow of lode blossom rock on its northern slope, made only a slight impression on him. He was after that elk.

It was wild, desolate country—just the kind of country that appealed to Conger's hunting instincts.

Conger fingered a piece of blossom rock as he lit his pipe. It was the fall of 1860.

Chapter Two

Scratch of the Pick

A WAR HAD BEEN FOUGHT, and the wounds, the hatreds and the deaths were still fresh in the mind.

The year was 1868.

Sam Conger was in Cheyenne (or Laramie…the accounts differ) that fall, strolling along the boardwalks near the freight depot, when his eye caught on a broken box of silver ore in transit over the Union Pacific railroad from the famous Comstock lode in Nevada.

"If that is silver ore," Conger thought, "I know where there is plenty of it."

His thought traced back to the blossom rock he had seen on the elk hunt in Colorado in 1860.

It was now fall and howling blizzards soon would turn the high country into blinding white deserts of snow and cold. There were blizzards in that high country that could snuff out a man's life as if it were but the flickering yellow flame of a miner's candle.

Only a fool…but the diggings were full of fools when it came to hunting for pay dirt.

Conger knew it would test the mettle of any man to face a timberline winter alone—but he had the prospectors' fever to keep him warm. Just at a time of year when most miners in the Gregory Diggings or in Russell's Gulch, a score of miles south of Caribou Hill, were packing their dust and heading for Denver City, Mexico, or the States, Conger headed for Caribou country.

When Conger walked between Caribou Hill and Idaho Mountain that fall he trudged over snow. The entire north slope of the hill was covered by large drifts. But Conger tramped on doggedly. During those early winter days, when he wasn't hunting or carrying wood to his campsite, he was rooting into the rocks of Caribou Hill. So it went the entire winter. Often it was more a battle for life than a battle for silver ore.

One day in the spring his heart skipped a beat. He discovered some traces of the blossom rock again. He surveyed the vast expanse of mountainside and determined that more eyes and more hands could search for the mother lode more profitably.

The search became an effort of six men—a prospecting party made up of Conger and two of his Central City friends, George Lytle and William Martin, who were partially grubstaked with supplies and tools by three ranchers, Hugh McCammon, John H. Pickel, and Samuel Mishler.

Martin was a Britisher who had trekked the Oregon Trail and had mined in southern California and at the Comstock.

George Lytle (left) was one of the co-discoverers of the Caribou lode in 1869. This portrait was from a charcoal drawing. Leonidas (Leo) Donnelly (center) was a pioneer of Caribou and briefly served as the mining camp's postmaster in 1876. When he arrived in the fall of 1870 he opened a store in a tent, which he was able to replace with a more permanent building in just a few months. Amos Bixby (right) edited the Caribou Post newspaper and later was the owner and editor of the Boulder County News from 1873 to 1878. He also served as Boulder postmaster in the 1880s.

Carnegie Library for Local History, Boulder

Lytle, at 44 years of age, had prospected and mined in the Cariboo district of British Columbia. It was he who later gave the new find its name of "Cariboo City." Mishler was his son-in-law.

The concentrated search began in August 1869, and on the thirty-first day of that month the find was made. It was on that day that the scratch of a prospector's pick opened up the fabulous Caribou Mine which would produce $8,000,000 in silver ore—one of the greatest silver mines in Colorado.

Most historians writing at that time agree that the first scratch was not made by Conger, although he had been the guiding force.

The Rocky Mountain Directory and Colorado Gazetteer for 1871 credits the Caribou find to Martin and Lytle, although pointing out that Conger found the first float. Various claims have later been made as to whether Martin or Lytle actually found the lode. Frank Fossett, one of Colorado's most eminent early historians, credits them both, and his report is corroborated by Amos Bixby, writer for the Caribou newspaper and author of a competent early history of Boulder and Clear Creek counties. These men were just a few years away from the event, and their accounts must be considered with respect.

They report that Conger found an outcropping higher on the hill, a vein which became the Poorman mine.

The final facts are that all six men shared the Caribou Mine equally. Later Conger traded his one-sixth interest in the Caribou lode for the entire right of his partners in the Poorman.

It was a joyous group of six men who packed supplies up to Caribou for the winter 1869-70. They built a winter cabin and packed in supplies on their backs.

Before winter set in, they cut a road through the forest and took one wagon load of ore to Professor Nathaniel Hill's smelting works at Blackhawk. All winter they worked, in the midst of howling blizzards, and piled up ore around the prospect hole.

They tried to be tight-lipped, but Central City and Blackhawk prospectors spotted the new silver ore and trailed the wagons back to Caribou.

In June of 1870 speculators rushed into the Caribou country. In less than a hundred days, 100 miners were on the spot. In another month there were three stores, one saloon, and two boarding houses. Caribou City was organized and platted September 26 in that first full year of its existence.

During those first few months in the summer of 1870 a typical boom camp grew in the valley just east of Caribou Hill. Many of the prospectors camped under the trees, in brush houses, or in tents until log cabins and frame buildings, stores, and hotels could be erected.

The road up Boulder Canyon was completed just three weeks before Fernando Cortez Willett traveled in 1871 from Boulder to Nederland (then known as Brownsville) and Caribou. In the photo on the right, a man stands between the road and the creek, near one of the road's 33 bridges below Dome Rock. It is believed that these images were taken by photographer Robert Lawrence Thompson in the early 1870s, and were part of a portfolio Willett sent back to his brother in Iowa.

Carnegie Library for Local History, Boulder

A toll collector's story

By R. E. Arnett

It wasn't possible to survey the road up Boulder Cañon during the summer because the water was too high through the Narrows, so they waited until the creek was frozen over during the winter and then surveyed the road from Nederland down over the ice. The road was finished about the latter part of July 1874 as I remember.

The road was then opened as a toll. Every day about 40 or 45 four-horse and six-horse freight teams, loaded with ore, lumber, posts, and poles arrived in Boulder. Two six-horse Concord stage coaches also arrived from Caribou every day, loaded up to the guards, some even riding on top, besides livery and private rigs coming into Boulder. All these freight wagons and other conveyances would return to the hills loaded with hay, grain groceries, powder, fuse, and all kinds of merchandise and supplies for the people in the hills.

The toll road became a paying proposition for its builders for a time.

Along about 1877, I was made toll gatekeeper and toll collector. It was a lonely place for a young man of 17, especially at night.

One of the stockholders would come up every two weeks to collect the toll money. Sometimes I would have two or three hundred dollars on hand which I would hide under the floor, and being a little leery at night of being held up I would leave the gate open during the late night and let the traffic go by.

The next gatekeeper, a Mr. Creese, who came after me, was also a little nervous about holdups, so he got a spoke out of a wagon wheel and strapped it on his wrist every time he went out to collect toll. Sure enough, he was held up one night. He gave one of the thugs (there were two) a rap over the head with the spoke and felled him...

In addition to collecting tolls, I had a horse and a two-wheel dump cart. Every day I was supposed to go over the road and fill up the chuck holes and bad places in order to keep the road passable. I wore a cap labeled "toll collector" and would take the toll as anyone passed by.

—Published in The Boulder Daily Camera on March 23, 1944

During that exciting summer of 1870, many rich finds were made at boom town Caribou. Among them was the Idaho, from which the finders realized over $6,000 in one month's sinking of the first 20 feet of shaft.

Others were the Trojan, Boulder County, Sovereign People, Spencer, No-Name, and the Seven Thirty.

Subsequently discovered were the Anchor, Belcher, Comstock, Crown Point, Centennial, Dutch Park, Eagle Bird, Tehel, Eureka, Fred Albrect, Grand View, Grant County, Idaho, Isabella, Mignon, Monitor, Montecarlo, Mount Vernon, Native Silver, Ontario, Potosi, Perigo, Rose of Killarney, Sherman, Shoshone, Silver Point, Single Jack, St. Louis, Stranger, Home Sweet Home, and the Up-To-Date.

Freight for Caribou was hauled up Boulder Cañon by large teams of horses.

Nederland Area Historical Society

Quite the boys

By J.C. (Charlie) Smith

While much has been said, down the through the years, about the mines in the Caribou district little has been said about the many freighters or teamsters, who were "quite the boys" in the early days.

They generally had four-horse outfits; some had six. Some were mule outfits and some were mixed—horse wheelers and mule leaders. Heavy loads of ore were hauled down to Boulder, and provisions, machinery, horse feed, etc., hauled back. Freight rates from Boulder were $1 per hundred pounds.

Mine timbers and wood for mine and mill boilers were also hauled by these large freight outfits.

A teamster, to let other outfits know he was ahead of them, had numerous little bells on the harness which rang merrily whenever a horse moved. Each teamster had a dog, which would run ahead, as dogs do, and would also announce his owner's approach.

These outfits, with their long rows of red white and blue harness rings, tinkling bells, plumes, and dyed horse-hair decorations were always an inspiring sight, especially to the younger generation. So much so that we boys were always ready to pick up a new word from any teamster's vocabulary.

The wagons had narrow tires, with another steel tire shrunk over the first, making them double-tired. They all had brakes, of which the brake-blocks (the part that rubbed against the wheel) had to be renewed every few days.

Some places the roads were so steep and the loads, especially of mining timbers, were so heavy that they would chain the wheels together over the load so the wagon wheels would slide instead of turn, which was very hard on the wheels. This was called roughlocking and was done to keep the wagon from running up on the wheel horses.

Several times, in bad blizzards, teamsters had to cut the tugs loose from the harness when the Devil's Elbow, a point one and a half miles below town was reached, as the wind strikes here with all its fury and the men felt they would perish if they tried to continue on into town in the wagons. By cutting the horses loose, they could ride a wheel-horse into town and all would reach there safely.

—Published in The Boulder Daily Camera in 1944

A horse trough was hewed out of a big pine log by John Heine in 1904, according to stories by Charlie Smith that were published in The Boulder Daily Camera in 1944 and in 1960. Charlie remembered, "The water came from a tunnel running back in the hill above the road." Charlie's brother Bill recollected that, "Teamsters used to come up here, let their horses drink that ice-cold water. They'd go over there [nearby grass], roll over and sometimes die." Charlie remembered that the town's old well was 60 feet deep, right in the center of town. "We didn't like the taste of its swampy water, so we went to the old horse trough and carried water." Charlie and his brother spent much of their boyhoods in Caribou.

Nederland Area Historical Society, Kemp Collection

In this street scene in 1883, men sit on the balcony railing where dances were held above Murphy's meat market. Next door is the Colorado House, a hotel.

Denver Public Library Special Collections, Z-12098

"In the year 1870," comments Bixby in his Boulder County history, "the opening of the rich Caribou silver mines pressed upon the business men of Boulder the importance of a wagon road direct from their town to Caribou."

The three businessmen were Maj. J.F. Buttles, Anthony Arnett, and Amos Widner. [Other accounts credit Arnett, Widner, and William Pound.] The road was opened by late January 1871. Four and six-mule teams hauled their heavy loads of provisions, machinery, feed, and ore in and out of the town. The rate to Boulder: $1 per hundred pounds.

Horses were trained, especially the leaders, in swinging out on the short turns so as not to pull the wagon off the narrow road. Their drivers put bells on the harnesses so that other wagon masters could hear them coming. Different teamsters were known by the sound of the bells echoing through the canyons. The road to Boulder had many steep pitches, and brake blocks had to be renewed on the wagons every few days. It was often necessary to "rough-lock" a heavy load by chaining the rear wheels so that they would slide.

Caribou becomes a town

A lot happened in Caribou in the year 1870. In July a pioneer business establishment opened—Van and Tilney groceries and provisions. Prescott W. Pierce opened the first meat market, and erected the first frame building in the town. Leo Donnelly, who had his store in a tent, began selling groceries and provisions in August. Within a few months he had replaced the tent with a substantial building.

When General U.S. Grant visited Central City in 1872 he walked from his carriage to the doorway of the Teller House on silver bricks produced by the Caribou Mine and photographed for this stereograph card.

New York Public Library, public domain

Men unload a wagon at a side entrance to the Sherman House Hotel, the large white structure in the center right, about 1880. The road that continues uphill around the right

corner of the hotel was Potosi Street, with most of the town's businesses. The white building in the lower left with the poles that braced it against the wind was the schoolhouse.

Nederland Area Historical Society, Clark Collection

Sears and Werley put up a billiard hall and advertised "three good tables." The building was a two-story structure, with upper rooms used for offices. Maj. E.M. Beard was proprietor of a saloon and boarding house in a 20-by-34-foot building built mostly by his own hands.

Many eastern capitalists were attracted by stories out of Caribou. On September 21, 1870, A.D. Breed, of Cincinnati, paid $50,000 cash for one-half of the Caribou Mine. The mine yielded about $70,000 that season, proving the purchase well worthwhile.

By the spring of 1871 there were about 60 substantial buildings in Caribou, and the population was about 400. It wasn't long before business houses crowded Potosi Street for a distance of 1,200 feet.

Peddler's wagon

By J.C. (Charlie) Smith

The greatest joy to us kids and also to the women folks was when the peddler's wagon came to town every week in the summer time with fresh vegetables, melons, and fruit.

If he got to the boarding houses first, where he naturally would go to sell the largest amount of his load at one time, the proprietress would buy so much of it, as she always had a large number of boarders, that it made it hard on other women, so they planned to meet the wagon below town as to be able to have a chance to get their share of his load before he reached the boarding houses.

—*Published in The Boulder Daily Camera in 1944*

Abel D. Breed purchased the west half of the Caribou Mine in 1870 for $50,000, and he bought the other half a year later. He built a 10-stamp mill in Caribou called the Caribou Mill, and in 1871 he constructed a second Caribou Mill at Brownsville (now Nederland) on Middle Boulder Creek. Here he pours coffee from a silver coffee service made from silver from his mine, which was one of the richest silver producers of its time. Just three years after he bought it, Breed sold the mine to a group of investors from Holland for $3 million, half of which he received in stock and half in cash.

Nederland Area Historical Society

The town's newspaper, the Caribou Post, with Collier and Hall of Central City as its founders, was established in the spring of 1871. It was published until August of the following year. Amos Bixby edited the Post.

As the influx of miners continued, Caribou's fabulous silver production got into full swing. In January of 1871 the Caribou shaft was 200 feet deep. In 1872 and 1873 the mine yielded bountifully.

By the end of August 1871 Caribou boasted several hotels and boarding houses; two billiard halls; one restaurant; five grocery stores; three bakeries; four saloons; one dry goods store; one millinery shop; two blacksmith shops; one livery stable; one meat market; and one photographic gallery.

In 1872 the silver wealth of the Caribou Mine was made especially notable by a walk of silver bricks, the product of

The original Caribou claim was developed by seven shafts, 100 feet apart, east and west along the main lode. The principal shaft was 1,040 feet deep with levels at intervals of 70 feet. The tunnel was 700 feet long, penetrating the north side of Caribou Hill, and cut the vein at the 300-foot level. Most of the ore ran in streaks and in masses, but some nuggets of pure silver were found.

Caribou folk pose for a photograph in front of Pete Werley's saloon.

Nederland Area Historical Society

the mine, extending from the carriage in the street to the doorway of the Teller House at Central City, laid for Gen. U.S. Grant to walk in on at the time of his visit to the city.

In 1872 Mr. Breed built a reducing mill on Middle Boulder Creek at the site of the present town of Nederland, about five miles east of Caribou. The following year he sold the Caribou property to "Gentlemen of The Hague, Holland" for $3,000,000. One half was paid for in stock and the remainder in cash. Breed received $1,000,000 and the first original Caribou owners about $165,000 each. The remainder went to other shareholders—Messrs. Cutter, Anker, Shaffenburg and others.

The Nederland Mining Co., as the new association was called, with Van Diest, Anker, and Prince as agents, did not prosper. After bad management, selfish purposes, and legal complications had their run, the sheriff passed the property over to the Hon. Jerome B. Chaffee and David H. Moffat on Sept. 15, 1876. Chaffee and Moffat paid $70,100 for the property. With Eben Smith in charge of operations the mine paid well for the next decade. The company maintained a payroll of $12,000 to $15,000 per month.

In 1874 the mine produced 1,800 tons of ore valued at $130,000, in 1875 $210,703, and in 1876 about $25,000 worth. The mine's average yield in 1875 was only $69.49 per ton, far from high grade and not equal to some mines in the district. But the Caribou produced quantity—more than all other Boulder County silver mines combined.

The Caribou vein crevice varied from three to twelve feet in depth, and pay ore from six to 36 inches in width. Records show that ores from the mine treated at the Nederland mill from 1871 to 1876 averaged 60 to 70 ounces per ton and the high grades from 200 to 20,000 ounces. In the year 1881 for example, $227,982.88 in silver bricks was sent through the Boulder express office, all of it from the company's mill, an amalgamation and chloridization plant at Nederland.

Chapter Three

Where the Winds Were Born

On July 9, 1875, the Caribou Silver Cornet Band, directed by Mr. Moyle, played a concert in Boulder.

Caribou was a town of possibly as many as 1,000 inhabitants[*] in that year of peak mineral production, when more than $200,000 in ores came from its mines.

There was a thriving business district.

The people of Caribou held parties and celebrations. They scoured the mountainsides for wild raspberries, strawberries, black currants, red currants, thimbleberries, and huckleberries. They were blessed with good drinking water and an awe-inspiring view of the mountains and plains, all with one sweep of the eye.

---

[*]The census of 1880 counted 549 residents in Caribou. Population estimates have gone as high as 3,000 people in the mid-1870s, but that number seems unlikely. At its peak, many of Caribou's miners lived in tents, and they probably were not counted in the census, so it seems possible that there could have been as many as 1,000 people living in the mining camp during its glory years.

The Caribou Silver Cornet Band in the 1870s.

Nederland Area Historical Society, Buchanan Collection

Talk to the people who used to live in Caribou. They'll tell about the first snows that sifted across Old Baldy. Or about the iron dike of magnetic rock, running north and south through town, which was struck repeatedly by lightning. The loss of livestock on the dike was heavy.

During storms, they said, walking in rubber boots could cause wobbly knees because of static electricity in the man's system. Children in the school building were startled when a spark jumped at them from the slate blackboard.

Winds blow in Caribou?

"Well," they will say, "we used to call it the place where the winds were born. When the wind blew at Nederland, the people there would say that someone at Caribou must have left his doors open."

The wind that blew at Caribou even gave rise to tall stories.

"Every spring you'd find the bones of some poor coyote laying alongside the mill houses, always on the west side. Wind'd blow so hard it would catch the poor critter up agin' the side of the building and hold him there 'til he'd starve to death."

There were two Cornish "Cousin Jack" miners in Pete Werley's saloon one day. One said he hadn't been in Caribou more than a couple of months and thought the climate was terrible. Always so cold, he complained.

The Caribou schoolhouse was buttressed against the ever-present wind.

Nederland Area Historical Society

"How long does winter last here?" he queried.

"Don't know," the other Cousin Jack replied. "I've only been here three years myself."

There were true stories about the winters.

Daddy Yates said that when he went to work in the Caribou Mine on the night shift he always left his shovel leaning

> ## When weather was weather
>
> There were very few plastered houses in Caribou in our day, and tar-paper was used under the sheeting to keep out the snow which sifted through every crevice and melted and ran down the walls, marring the wallpaper.
>
> Our house was in a rather sheltered place, just the location for a drift to form and cover the kitchen door all winter. It was impossible to keep it clear of snow if we used the front door, and by the time spring arrived there was a nice snow room formed by digging out the tightly packed snow and melting it for the family laundry. It took Monday for melting snow and straining the water and we washed on Tuesdays. As the miners worked ten hours a day and sawed and split wood for the fires in the evening after work, the melting of snow for laundry purposes saved the men some labor in carrying water from the well.
>
> The windows of the houses had four panes of glass in each sash, and only the upper sash of our kitchen window could be cleared in winter. My husband shoveled the snow out every morning, and often I was obliged to clear it away during the day. One day an extra hard gust of wind took me off my feet and the shovel flew out of my hands straight through a precious pane of glass and on to the floor inside the house, frightening the baby in his high chair. As this one was the third pane broken while shoveling snow that winter, it was quite a calamity.
>
> —Published in The Boulder Daily Camera in 1929, author unknown

The Potosi Street business district was thriving in this re-touched 1870s photograph. On the far left is Pete Werley's saloon. Men greatly outnumbered the women in the mining camp, and the only women in the photograph posed in front of the church across the street from Werley's. The telegraph office, which also housed the police court, is just beyond them, followed by Murphy's Meat Market which is decorated with antlers and had a dance hall with a balcony on its second floor.

Nederland Area Historical Society, Buchanan Collection

Caribou's buildings were always in danger of blowing apart in the fierce winter winds that blew through town from the Continental Divide. Residents used poles to buttress their homes and businesses, and they cut down a lot of trees for firewood to keep the fires going to heat homes

and power mine equipment. Hardly any trees survived in the wake of Caribou's boom, and today none of the buildings remain, replaced by a lush, peaceful meadow.

Nederland Area Historical Society

against a tree on the trail so the next morning he could open up the tunnel to his cabin door, which had drifted full of snow during the night.

Following each snowstorm he would put on an additional link of stovepipe to keep the pipe above the drifts so the stove would draw. The pipe was anchored to nearby trees to keep it from blowing down.

100 percent heroes

By J.C. (Charlie) Smith

Blizzards were a terror to the doctors who had patients in Caribou. I remember when my brother, Hugh, was born, Feb. 12, 1906, the late Dr. Carbon Gillapsie, who had offices in Nederland from the fall of 1905 until the fall of 1908, was my mother's physician. He came from Nederland in a bad storm, and after my brother was born and he went to get into his carriage to go home, the horse bolted and ran away, scattering the rig and instruments among the stumps and rocks over quite a bit of the town.

Dr. Carbon Gillaspie

The cause of the horse's fright was the long shadows cast by the lantern my father had hung on the back of the buggy in order that the doctor might see to drive home. My father finally caught the horse, and Dr. Gillaspie had to lead the horse and walk the four miles back to Nederland through the blinding blizzard and darkness. He would not stay overnight as he said that someone else might need his services.

These doctors, who rode horseback or in rigs over the old-time roads in the mountains through blizzards, thunderstoms and windstorms, were the 100 percent heroes of that time.

—Published in The Boulder Daily Camera on January 21, 1944

Businesses on Potosi Street in the mid-'70s

North side
- Caribou Boarding House
- across Brewery Street coming east, Pete Werley's saloon (above on left)
- post office and Johnny Simmons' dry goods store
- Scott Bros. general store
- the open lot with the spring that supplied Caribou's water
- Herzinger and Harter general store, later run by Joe Loyd
- Hughes saloon
- Rhimer candy store
- shaft house of the Potosi mine
- three residences
- Shoo-Fly dance hall
- Jennie Graham's establishment, next door to another run by her sister, Anna
- followed by a row of residences

South side
- Community church
- Murphy's meat market
- Colorado Hotel
- Newell boarding house and saloon
- a residence
- Dobson's saloon
- three residences
- the $50,000 Sherman House hotel

In 1944, shortly before her death, Grandma Harris remarked: "There isn't a human being alive that can face those Caribou blizzards without protection. You had to cover your face to breathe—and it was a matter of crawling through the blizzard, not walking against it."

She remembered times when the miners crawled on hands and knees against the gale.

Late one July, she said, a three-inch snowfall brought a quick end to a picnic in the nearby mountains.

Caribou residents stuffed cloth into the keyholes of their outside doors. If they didn't, there would be a bushel of snow on the floor in the morning.

"We would be entirely snowed in almost every morning," she said. "The wind drifted the snow above the windows.

So many berries

By J.C. (Charlie) Smith

The rainfall was much heavier in the early days than it has been for many a year. Raspberries, strawberries, black currants, red currants, thimbleberries, and hackberries grew everywhere around Caribou. The huckleberries, which still grow there, but not so plentifully, are the same kind as grown on the tundra in the Hudson Bay region, I'm told.

Women of the town picked and canned large quantities of these berries so their cellars were full of jams, jellies, and berries every winter. These were a treat after eating dried apples and peaches, which were used extensively.

—Published in The Boulder Daily Camera in 1944

The Up To Date mine was one of the first to be opened in Caribou. When this photo was taken in 1912 a newspaper said that some claimed the mine was the best developed in the state. The mine may have been mostly exploratory with little production, but they didn't skimp on their signage and promotion.

Denver Public Library Special Collections, Z6329

Father would shovel us out, then it was my job to clear the drifts away from some of the windows. No door could fit tight enough to keep the snow from sifting in."

Her father, superintendent of the Caribou Mine, owned the finest house in Caribou, a house that stands yet [in 1957] in twisted dilapidation. William and Eliza Todd built the home in the fall of 1876. Their daughter, "Grandma Harris" was married in the house to William Harris on Christmas day, 1882. There was a sumptuous banquet after the ceremony, and then the guests and wedding party adjourned to the Murphy dance hall where the celebration continued until morning.

William and Eliza Todd built their home in Caribou in 1876 when William was the superintendent of the Caribou Mine. It became a boarding house in its later years and survived fires and earthquakes before it was abandoned and gradually faded away.   *Nederland Area Historical Society, Buchanan Collection*

The Sherman House was a huge three-story building at the east edge of the business district. During some of the worst winters there was a snowbank level with the upstairs windows, through which guests entered and departed. It was jokingly referred to as the Sherman House elevator. The elevator was in full operation during the winter of 1875-76 when snow fell steadily for seventeen days and nights.

Uncle Billy Donald was proprietor of the Sherman House for many years. People will tell you that was a place to get a meal. The steaming food seemed especially inviting if wind and snow swirled outside the frosted windows.

Potosi Street was lined on both sides with business houses, but the Sherman House was Caribou's gathering place.

Caribou had four streets running east and west. At the north was Main Street, next Potosi, the third was Jones, and the fourth Quigley. One north-south street was Sherman, which ran immediately east of the Sherman House. Another to the west of the business district was Brewery Street.

The Potosi mine, shown here in the early 1930s, was the only mine in city limits. It closed after its initial success during Caribou's boom years and was reopened in 1889, only to be hampered by water seepage. It suspended operation two years later in 1891 when an apparent stock promotion failed.

Denver Public Library Special Collections, X-61531

> # Not only Cornishmen
> *By J.C. (Charlie) Smith*
>
> Many people think of the old-time mining men of the county as mostly Cornishmen. There were more Cornish people than other nationalities, but there were also Norwegians, Swedes, Irish, Swiss, Finns, and a few Missourians who were starting to venture away from their homes. These old timers were very good people and went out of their way to help one another.
>
> —Published in The Boulder Daily Camera in 1944

Cousin Jack and Cousin Jenny

Many of Caribou's residents were Cousin Jacks, who learned their mining trade in the copper and tin mines of Cornwall, England. They were needed in Caribou to unlock the rich veins of silver ore. Origin of the terms "Cousin Jack" and "Cousin Jenny" seems uncertain. But one historian writes that the term originated in Caribou when a resident remarked: "If you ask one Cornish miner who his friend is, he'll say: Oh that's my Cousin Jack, just over from the old country."

Songs of the Cousin Jacks brought warmth to the lonely and windswept mountainsides. If two Cousin Jacks were within hearing distance of each other there was a duet. If there were more, there was a chorus. At Christmas time the mine shafts and tunnels echoed with Cornish voices blended into carol singing. On the Fourth of July they opened a keg of beer and sang far into the night.

They couldn't be excelled in single-jacking—hammering a steel drill into the hard granite preparatory to setting a dynamite charge.

They went to Cornwall for their brides, and they sang and danced all night after the wedding. They sang to the painted ladies on Potosi and lower Idaho streets, and they sang as they carried their departed up the winding hill to the cemetery.

They were a superstitious people, their imaginations fed by a folklore that was spawned in the legendary background of Cornwall. Women in a mine meant bad luck. Whistling in a mine was bad luck. Rats in a mine meant good luck because, they reasoned, rats can smell poisonous gases and won't stay in a mine where there is bad air. If they saw an unusually large gathering of birds as they walked to the mine they turned around and went home for a day off. If a bird perched too near them they took the day off. They told about small imps, "Tommy Knockers," who inhabited the mines. If anyone bothered these creatures that brought on back luck. The "Tommy Knocker" rattled rocks onto the hardboiled hats, misplaced their hammers, put a puddle of water in an unexpected spot.

The Cousin Jacks introduced into Colorado's mining lore the Cousin Jack pasty, saffron cake, and tea. The pasty was their most important dish—a delicately balanced mixture of potatoes, onions, and meat rolled in dough and baked in the oven.

The Cousin Jacks carried on a constant rivalry with the Irish miners, and sometimes that rivalry was argued out with bared fists.

Many of the Cousin Jacks remained single men, isolated from their homeland. They financed presents for Caribou youngsters at the annual Christmas party in the church. Each child spoke a "piece," and in return received dolls, a sack of candy, cookies, fruit, and nuts. Each boy got a book.

This the Cousin Jack did on $3 per day for an eight-hour shift.

Chapter Four

The Boom and The Bust

Silver dribbling from its pockets, Caribou tossed its cap into the air, whooped, and clicked its heels together. It was digging silver that later graced the dinner tables of America, or dangled as an ornament from the necks of beautiful ladies of the East.

There was something about the hard rock, the icy gales, the wind, snow, and lightning that became an alchemy to produce stout hearts. The people of Caribou sat around their cherry-red cookstoves and wondered how there could possibly be a better life than this.

But in Washington, D.C., in the halls of Congress, whiskered gentlemen who knew more about international finance than they did about mining sat behind their legislative desks and talked about silver dollars.

Free coinage of silver was abolished, and the price of the metal started a decline.

Men unload logs from a wagon at a mine in Caribou sometime between 1890 and 1910.
Denver Public Library Special Collections, X-61533

The Caribou Mine shaft house in the 1890s. The men standing in front of the doors are dwarfed by the massive building. *Nederland Area Historical Society, Buchanan Collection*

The people of Caribou paused momentarily to hold their breath, confused and transfixed, as if they heard a gunshot and a scream in the middle of a dance.

Yet despite demonetization in 1873, Caribou's boom continued.

Hotels were crowded with guests in August of 1873. Breed had just sold his mine for $3,000,000. The Caribou Mine produced $130,000 in 1874. On October 6, 1874, the Boulder County Commissioners granted a petition to incorporate the town of Caribou. During the previous month the newspapers reported that sixty new buildings had been built there during the summer season.

In 1875 the Caribou Mine produced $210,703. The year 1875 was the peak production year, and the peak of Caribou's population. In 1876 a display of Caribou silver ore at the Centennial Exposition in Philadelphia drew nationwide attention to the silver capital. The magnificent display drew another influx of people to the silver mines.

The Caribou wasn't the only heavy producer of silver ore. The Poorman, Sam Conger's find, was one of the best. In 1874 and 1875 it produced 152 tons of ore for which $21,504 was paid at Blackhawk, Golden, and Nederland. In 1876, however, the yield dropped markedly. The Poorman vein was no more than one or two feet wide. The operation was saved solely by the high grade of the ore.

Some of the richest ore found at Caribou came from the Sherman mine. There the vein was only six to twelve inches wide. In 1876, 300 tons of ore with an average value of $270 per ton was sold to Boston and Colorado smelting works.

The Belcher Mine in the 1890s.

Nederland Area Historical Society, Flarty Collection

Most of the mines in the region produced well. Mrs. Newell, wife of a saloon keeper, believed she could laugh at the experienced miners and geologists, and started across the hill one day to "witch" a mine in the same manner as she "witched" water wells. She opened the Wigwam shaft, slightly beyond the main silver belt. The mine was never a heavy producer.

Caribou residents had money to spend—lots of it. Few held on to it very long, although many of those that did used it to develop gold and tungsten mines in this region later. Sons of those men are still mining in Boulder County.

The big mill at Nederland produced many silver bricks for the mint at Denver. Rumbling ore wagons, with their loads of silver treasure, stirred the dust of the "Coon Trail" road between Caribou and Cardinal, and then on to Nederland, Boulder, Central City, Blackhawk, Golden, and Denver.

The town was served by daily mail from Boulder, and tri-weekly from Central City. W.L. Smith's stages ran between Caribou, Central City, and Boulder.

The Denver, Boulder and Western railroad touched Cardinal, only two miles east of Caribou. It was said that Caribou taxes built the Boulder County courthouse.

The effect of demonetization began to be felt. The pressure was temporarily relieved when Congress passed the Sherman Silver Purchase Act in 1890 to raise the price of silver above $1 an ounce.

Miners sort ore inside a shafthouse on Caribou Hill.
Denver Public Library Special Collections, K272

A national financial panic in 1893 caused widespread distress, and a dollar-conscious Congress repealed the Sherman Act to strike silver mining a final paralyzing blow.

William Jennings Bryan, a silver-throated orator from Nebraska, brought cheers and brief hope to the stunned silver miners. On August 16, 1893, he made an impassioned plea to defeat the bill repealing the Sherman Act. His words carried down through the ensuing decade when mining interests attempted to achieve free coinage of silver again.

Summoning all of his oratorical ability, Bryan shouted:

"You shall not press down upon the brow of labour this crown of thorns; you shall not crucify mankind upon a cross of gold."

Abandoned Caribou Mine buildings sometime between 1920 and 1940.

Denver Public Library Special Collections, X-61535

Hoisting equipment inside the shafthouse of the Caribou Mine after it closed down, probably in the 1940s.   *Nederland Area Historical Society, Kemp Collection*

He became the Democratic nominee for president. At the same time he obtained the nominations of the Populists and National Silver parties. In the campaign he traveled more than 18,000 miles and made 600 speeches in 27 different states, which was a record for that time. William McKinley, the Republican candidate, defeated him by 271 electoral votes to 176.

In 1908 the Democratic national convention was held in Denver, and Bryan was again nominated. (He had been nominated also in 1900.) As far as the nation itself was concerned, the free silver issue was dead. But western mining men carried silver-headed Bryan canes, and it was heresy to speak against the Nebraska Democrat. Unfortunately for them, Taft was destined to be the next president.

But to back up a little: the mid-1870s were prosperous for Caribou, despite demonetization. They were the years that led up to 1879. That year was an unlucky toss of the dice for the silver capital. The dice called for death and destruction.

Both came within a few months' period, and by early fall of that year Caribou had been dealt a blow from which it never fully recovered. Only a good price for silver would have brought it back.

'Remember friends as you pass by'

High on a saddle to the north of Caribou where one can look to the setting sun of the west, across a sweeping valley that is the lap of Old Baldy mountain, and high where the wind never ceases to blow and where the snow piles high in the wintertime, Caribou buried its dead.

The view of Old Baldy peak from Caribou's cemetery, unknown date.
Nederland Area Historical Society, Glenna Carline Collection

The Caribou cemetery when many of the headstones were still intact.
Nederland Area Historical Society, Buchanan Collection

The cemetery is a beauty spot in the summertime, a playground for snowstorms in the winter—a lot like Caribou itself.

Stories of two epidemics of scarlet fever and diphtheria are written in the stone and wooden grave markers. On the 14 markers still readable, seven of the deaths were in 1879.

Take this stone that is still standing [in 1957]:

*Willie, son of Samuel and Margaret Richards,
died July 6, 1879, 8 years, six months.
Anna 10 years, July 8.
Alice Mae, 3 years, July 15.*

How often has so much tragedy been told in words so few? That is a story filled with the tragedy of living and of dying—three children of one family taken in nine days.

The doctors and home medication failed. Influenza and diphtheria mocked applications of sage tea and mustard plasters, of onion poultices, and of generous swigs of kerosene and whiskey.

"Poor old Dr. Mann," Grandma Harris recalled. "He was sick himself, and it worried him so much when the epidemic began taking so many children. He was powerless to help. And those poor boys in the mines. We hardly knew some of them by name. Sometimes we put up a marker, but a lot of them will go unknown now."

Friends would bring them down from the mines, or from their cabins, and place them either in the Catholic or Protestant churches. A few people would gather. A prayer was said: a half dozen Cousin Jacks, caps in hand, would offer a hymn. Then the casket was carried up the hill to the cemetery, sometimes not to be buried until the frost left the ground in the spring. A rumble of dynamite blast now meant something else—it could be a mining operation, or it could be efforts to excavate a grave in the granite hillside.

"So many are gone," Grandma Harris recalled. In her Cornish accent she added: "So many were bah-rn, mah-ried and bah-ried in Caribou."

The cemetery has crumbled and decayed. Wooden fences around graves have rotted. Iron fences have rusted and twisted. Wooden markers have weathered until names are barely discernible. Stones have broken and fallen.

Sunken depressions are all that mark some graves. An aspen tree grows from the heart of one.

Here are some of the markers still readable [in 1957]:

James T. Williams, Oct. 1879, Age 30.

Frances Ann Pugh, June 7, 1880, 62 years, 3 mo., 15 days.

John, son of J.I. Retallach, age 4 years.

Emma, daughter of J. and E. George, 1877, Aug. 7, 9 years.

Sarah Collins, wife of James Collins, born in Cornwall, 36 years, died 1875, Oct. 5.

W.M. Hicks, Cornwall, died 1875, age 27.

Son of P. and E. Spanner... rest illegible.

Agnes Julia, daughter of Rev. Albert and Laura H. Ewert, 6 months, 1882.

Son of M.A. and I.G. Lunsford, April 30, 1878, 1 year, 15 days.

Darling Tommy, son of J. and M.A. Cosgrove, June 27, 1879, age 3 years, 5 months, 26 days.

Margaret, wife of Ed Perkins, died Jan. 3, 1879, age 45.

Almost all of the headstones in the Caribou cemetery were vandalized and disappeared over the years.

Nederland Area Historical Society, Edgeley W. Todd Collection

Men, women, and children died at Caribou. Strangely enough the cemetery—a symbol of death in the thriving days of Caribou—now is about all that is left as a symbol of life in that mining town. Headstones have endured where frame houses tumble in the path of capricious winds.

Wild weather born on the Continental Divide, a few miles to the west, is mocking even this human endeavor. The Caribou region is timberline country, and time will see the last vestiges of the people who lived there wiped out.

A horse and buggy climb up one of Caribou's streets around 1899.
Nederland Area Historical Society, Kemp Collection, photo by Harry H. Lake

> # A proper water system
>
> By J.C. (Charlie) Smith
>
> A water trough was cut out of a solid log by John Heyniee [Heine] in the summer of 1904. Water flowing into it is spring water piped from an old tunnel which had long been caved-in. This trough of water is a far-cry from the water system put in by townspeople when the town was first built. For they not only had the reservoir between the west end of town and the Caribou Mine, but had water mains and several fire plugs. Had this water system been kept in repair, the second fire could have been stopped before it did much damage; but by 1905, those pipes had rusted and fallen apart, so the old town, built of pitch boards, went up in smoke in about three hours' time.
>
> —Published in The Boulder Daily Camera in 1944

Devastating fires deal staggering blows

The year was still 1879, and the month September. Caribou had another ordeal to face.

For several weeks there had been forest fires in the region. The sky was murky with smoke.

One Sunday morning Caribou citizens noticed a red sky to the west of town. The spark had been touched by a campfire carelessly left smouldering. The wind rose to a gale and very soon fire was leaping through the trees. Mine buildings on the ridge west of town began to burn. A water supply protected the business district, but a water line below the Sherman House at the east edge of the business district was broken and no water was available in the lower end of town to fight the blaze.

Abandoned houses in Caribou sometime between 1920 and 1940.

Denver Public Library Special Collections, X-6810

The remains of Caribou from Idaho Hill looking south as seen through the lens of photographer Don Kemp in the summer of 1939. The Potosi Mine buildings (including today's stone ruins) are at left. The dilapidated remains of the Caribou School House are in the right center, still buttressed by poles against winter's raging winds. The wooded ridge of Goat Mountain is at right center. On the skyline are Mounts Thorodin and Tremont.

Denver Public Library Special Collections, K-18

The fire skipped over the central business district, but ate away almost every structure east of the Sherman House.

It didn't take long. Many homes, mine buildings and valuable machinery were burned. Long rows of wood corded for winter use were a total loss.

An account of the fire, written by Mrs. Mary Collins, whose husband was James Collins, a pioneer of the Caribou camp, as printed in the April 28, 1922, edition of the Boulder News-Herald, said:

"I learned that the lower street of the town was on fire and that the Caribou Mine building was burning. There were known to be four men in the mine who would be smothered unless they could be rescued. I turned to see the wife of one of them who was my friend, and I shall never forget the look of horror and despair in her face. My sister Julia and her three tiny children were with us also and everyone seemed to be panic stricken, the fire had come down so suddenly.

"My husband soon appeared and started for the mine to ascertain whether Mr. A—and the other men had escaped. He met them running down the hill, and our fears as to their safety were soon relieved, but they had a narrow escape. The signal to come up had been given them as soon as the danger had been realized. The engineer stood at his post with the flames roaring around him until the men had all stepped from the bucket uninjured as the great rope above them was smoking."

And from Grandma Harris: "Father and our neighbors covered our house with wet blankets in order to keep the sparks from igniting it. But we were lucky, because the main body of the fire didn't cross the ridge into our area."

In later years Caribou residents looked back on this hour of tragedy and recalled two humorous incidents.

One man dashed into his home. A minute later he was at an upstairs window, which he threw open. In one hand he held a big mirror, in the other a flatiron. He hesitated a moment, then threw out the mirror, which shattered into a thousand pieces. He carried the flatiron safely out-of-doors.

Another man ran out his front door with a big can of kerosene. He unscrewed the cap and poured the oil out on the ground right next to his home. Then he grabbed a shovel and buried the can.

The fire was a staggering blow.

By 1880 Caribou's population had dwindled to 549 people, and by 1890 there were only 169 residents. Full effects of the demonetization of silver were also taking their toll. Many of the mines were shut down.

The town tried to rebuild and did a fair job of it. But many of the miners headed for the boom camp of Leadville. In 1893 came the final blow, with repeal of the Sherman Act.

A few residents hung on.

It was on December 26, 1899, that a final blow was struck at Caribou when a fire raged through the downtown district. Many of the store buildings, vacant at the time, were destroyed.

As smoke drifted out of the ruins, the few residents of the town who had formed a bucket brigade found that all they

Caribou declined further after the final fire in the winter of 1905-1906. By the mid-1940s, only a few buildings were still standing.

Nederland Area Historical Society, Buchanan Collection

Today, all that remains of the once booming mining camp are vestiges of its once bustling town streets, now hiking trails.

had been able to save was the church, the Sherman House, and the hotel belonging to William McDonald.

The year 1900 saw gold production reach a peak at Cripple Creek, Colorado, far to the south of Caribou. With an average production of about $20,000,000 annually, Cripple Creek drew miners from many Colorado camps, including Caribou.

In that year, Caribou reported a population of 44 people. There was one store in town.

The final blows: An earthquake and yet another fire

There were still two more touches to the destruction of Caribou, more stage effects than anything else. In 1903 an earthquake shook dishes from their cupboards, cracked plaster and disjointed stove pipe. Nature was almost sadistic in reaching so ridiculously into its bag of tricks to visit the town with an earth tremor.

The final destruction came in the winter of 1905-1906, when fire destroyed the most memorable structure of all, the Sherman House, and along with it the few remaining business structures. That fire burned lonesomely, because few Caribou residents remained to fight it.

There were 51 people living in Caribou in 1910, when a state mining bulletin reported that since its founding in 1869, Caribou had produced a total wealth of $20,000,000 in precious metals. In 1920 the population had slumped to 47 people, and in 1928 the town became merely an election precinct for Nederland.

Caribou's once proud mining structures eventually succumbed to the ravages of time.

Nederland Area Historical Society, Kemp Collection

EPILOGUE

1957

Caribou, like the Canadian reindeer which shares its name, pawed its food—silver—from beneath the frozen snow. The lifeblood of its silver veins pinched out and the town stumbled to a stop, and died.

Ever-blowing gales, furious rainstorms, and blizzards have polished white the bones of its carcass. The town "where the winds were born," as the miners called it, has succumbed to them.

Heavy wooden doors on the few remaining cabins swung for a while on rusty hinges and then tore loose. Shingles rattle on roofs and the winds howl through the broken windows of tottering frame houses.

No one lives there now.

In wintertime cabins are filled to their roof-tops—inside and outside—with snow. The timberline weather takes its toll every year in another cabin or two crushed down.

The wind drowns out the sound of laughter drifting down from the windows of the Shoo-Fly dance hall. It has torn down the shacks of the painted ladies on lower Idaho Street and muffles their dusky laughter. It has puffed out the kerosene lights that, of a night, cast flickering patches of yellow light on the boardwalks of Potosi Street.

The remaining mine buildings creak from age and not from the weight of fabulously rich silver ore hoisted in buckets from the cavernous shafts on Caribou Hill.

Only the spring, oozing ice-cold water, there before Caribou was, remains in the heart of what was the business district.

Timberline, the land of nothingness, remains. A pack rat or a chipmunk, scurrying through the ruins, are the living inhabitants of the town. The call of a bird falls on no human ear. In the fringe of life below timberline, twisted, gnarled trees—many gashed by lightning—fight for life. Their branches are twisted to the east, away from the perpetual wind, and their windward surfaces have become red, toughened bark.

Eventually, like the town of Caribou, they will tumble down.

Caribou was born in a wild country. It was a strong child. It led a tempestuous life, worked hard for its living, and in the twilight of its existence told a gripping story of mining in the West.

Finally, on the fringes of timberline, it lost its fight with the winds of time.

—John and Doris Buchanan

Today

A new preservation and restoration project was begun in 2022 for the Caribou Cemetery by the Friends of the Caribou Cemetery in conjunction with the Nederland Area Historical Society.

Friends of Caribou Cemetery

Most of the burials in the Caribou Cemetery date from 1875 through 1898, during Caribou's main period of mining activity. Many were miners who, with their families, traveled the seas from Cornwall to work in the silver mines. Some of the men died in mine accidents, and some of the women died during their childbearing years, while many of the children succumbed to scarlet fever and diphtheria.

Sadly, the cemetery became neglected and vandalized, and only a broken portion of one of the intricately carved historic gravestones remains intact.

In coordination with the Nederland Area Historical Society, community residents formed the "Friends of Caribou Cemetery" in 2022. The following year, the group cleaned up debris, re-fenced the perimeter, erected an arch over a new gate, and mapped the known and suspected burial sites. Upcoming plans include marking all known graves and installing two interpretive signs — one for the cemetery itself and one, on mining history, for the Caribou townsite.

The goal of the Friends group is to restore dignity and respect to the cemetery's men, women, and children. They are not forgotten.

Remember friends as you pass by,
As you are now, so once was I.
As I am now so you must be,
Prepare for death and follow me.

(Epitaph on the gravestone of Mary Webster, 1840-1879)

Houses and mines were still drifted in from winter's wind and snow when photographer and historian Don Kemp took this photograph in 1945, probably in the late spring.

Denver Public Library Special Collections, K–132

Bibliography

Baker, J.H., and Hafen, LeRoy, *"History of Colorado,"* State Historical Society of Colorado, Denver, 1927.

"Colorado, A Guide to the Highest State," American Guide Series, Hastings House, New York, 1941.

Fossett, Frank, *"Colorado, Its Gold and Silver Mines,"* C.G. Crawford, Printer and Stationer, New York, 1880.

Hall, Frank, *"History of the State of Colorado,"* Blakely Printing Co., Chicago, 1889.

Smith, Duane A., *"Silver Saga: The Story of Caribou, Colorado, Revised Edition,"* University Press of Colorado, Mining The American West Series, 2003.

Stone, Wilbur Fisk, *"History of Colorado,"* S.J. Clarke Publishing Co., Chicago, 1918.

Vickers, W.B. (editor), *"History of Clear Creek and Boulder Valleys, Colorado,"* O.L. Baskin and Co., Chicago, 1880.

Files of the Boulder Daily Camera, the Boulder County News, the Boulder News-Herald, the Caribou Post, Colorado Magazine, and The Trail.

Portions of this story on Caribou were prepared by the authors for use in 1944 by the Boulder Daily Camera. We are grateful to A.A. Paddock, editor of the Camera, for allowing us to use some of these materials again, and for supplying old pictures of the town of Caribou for use in this book.

www.ingramcontent.com/pod-product-compliance
Lightning Source LLC
Chambersburg PA
CBHW061814290426
44110CB00026B/2869